Jamie Thrasivoulou is an award-winning  lyricist and workshop facilitator from D⸺ ⸺ared in The Morning Star, P⸺ ⸺e, The Arsonist, Glove, Raz⸺ ⸺d Ink Zine and Bluecoat Pr⸺

His first collection, The⸺ ⸺d in May 2017 through Silh⸺

In 2017 Jamie was comm⸺ ⸺ed to write the poem 'A Privatised Map of Deprivation' for the award-winning photographer Jim Mortram's Small Town Inertia photography collection. The poem, along with work from Jim's collection, was displayed in the Small Town Inertia exhibition at Side Gallery in Newcastle.

Jamie is the official Derby County Football Club poet; his poem 'We Are Derby' is played on the big screen before every home game at Pride Park stadium. In 2018 he became the first poet to perform at the East Midlands derby between DCFC and Nottingham Forest, where he spat verse to over 31,000 people. He has since performed to over 33,000 against both Leeds United and West Bromwich Albion. 'We Are Derby' was played at Wembley stadium during the 2019 EFL Playoff Final.

Jamie won the 2019 Saboteur award for Best Spoken Word Performer, and the project Man Up, which he collaborated on with Restoke, received the award for Best Collaborative Work. In 2018 his musical project Bloque Capitals was joint winner of the Culture Matters: Bread and Roses award for spoken word and musical collaboration. In January 2019 Jamie was part of the UNISLAM 2019 winning team with the University of Birmingham.

He's currently the writer-in-residence at HMP Foston Hall. Jamie is also a visiting lecturer at Derby University.

Our Man

Jamie Thrasivoulou

Burning Eye

This edition published by Burning Eye Books 2019

www.burningeye.co.uk

@burningeyebooks

Burning Eye Books
15 West Hill, Portishead, BS20 6LG

ISBN 978-1-911570-68-4

Our Man

For Chops

CONTENTS

UNDERDOG CITY

SNAKES OF GREED

TAKEN INTO CONSIDERATION

MY HUMBLE ABODE

Welcome to my humble abode, a six-by-eight on Welford Road.

A smashed up, battered, shabby cell
of pre-Victorian sewerage smells.

Welcome to my humble abode, a six-by-eight on Welford Road.

My pad-mate's in for nicking fags,
and I've been gripped for dodging tax.

Welcome to my humble abode, a six-by-eight on Welford Road.

My brief he brings me glimmers of hope,
my defence somewhere in scrunched-up notes.
He recites to me in toffee tones
on how I'm to address the droves.
In stone-cold silence I raise a frown:
Not a chance, man. D'ya take me for a clown?
Them at the top've paid less than me.
I'll take my chance with an innocent plea.
So take your notes and leave me be
and apply for my bail hearing ASAP!

Welcome to my humble abode, a six-by-eight on Welford Road.

Where grown men fight to use the phones
and gangsters run rackets from their *wing*-zones.

Welcome to my humble abode, a six-by-eight on Welford Road.

And it's enough to make any man weep
when he reads the writing on his bail sheet!

Goodbye, farewell, my humble abode,
you six-by-eight on Welford Road.

I'd love to say I'll miss you so, but that'd be a lie;
that we both know.

#TERRACED STREET GAMES

Hopscotch the dog muck
amongst the autumn leaves,
avoid the stench
of rank stale bins.

SOMEONE'S LEFT BEHIND A SOVEREIGN RING…

I see you and you see me,
but there are black spots.
In the corner,
to the left of the pool table,
opposite the dartboard,

or in that seat by the window –
the one in which Stevie glassed that cockney youth,
right after he said,
I actually liked Thatcher!
all matter-of-factly.
Good old Stevie saw to him, mind!

Obviously there's the bogs as well;

both cubicles are guaranteed occupied on a weekend night,
the tiles still caked in tar from before the smoking ban.
Toilet tops littered with nefarious substances,
fast, ket, cat, ching.
Someone's even left behind a sovereign ring!

Back at the bar Murdoch-news-reading muppets
are rendered defeated and drunk-out for the day.
The monitor behind the bar details every word of crimes that pay!
Every utterance of knocked-off meat, deli cheese, HD tellies and
games consoles – chored and cheap, with no guarantee!
Stevie turns round to Bob the barman, and says,
Turn the fuckin' jukebox up – we can hear ourselves talk!

LIVING THE DREAM ROUTINE

wake up
mattress
sheetless
spunk-stained
attic room

springs in back
instead of steps

the afternoon birds
next door
are
mingin' out
the airwaves
with their
Spotify playlists

bad taste in choonz

rise up

walk past
pinholed
Coke can
makeshift
crack pipe

rocks in socks
behind wash piles

blackened ashtray
half-arsed
spliff
looks well loose!

pick up
smoke to get normal

brush teeth
shit, shower
walk dog
yam banana
go work
come home

repeat

YOOT

after 'Bullet Boy' by Miggy Angel

Yoot grown up in bruck-up council flat
Yoot learn tricks of trade from day-dot
Yoot nar learn ter read 'im learn ter shot
Yoot learn how ter mekk paper quick-time
Yoot soon stepz inter endz of nex-manz
Yoot be shottin' tingz on nex-manz turf
Yoot's soon hunted down in retribution
Yoot's last sentence was spat out in lead bars
Yoot thought he sussed game too young

now	Yoot	gone
just	a	twinkle
in	the	barrel
of	a	gun

TRAIN CRAWLER

Men and women of erudite knowledge
clash with selfie cool kids
for first-class seats.

I'm the bandit in the corner armed with a notebook.
I take down accents & dialogue.

I tune in to secret conversations
between husbands, wives and secret knock-offs at the end of
the line.

PLEASE WATCH YOUR STEPS:
THE SURFACES MAY BE SLIPPY!
anoints the station tannoy;
a ten-out-of-ten performance for observation!

MUCH LIKE THE SERVICES!
I declare abruptly from the corner
(which goes unacknowledged).

Folks are too immersed in their supermarket literature,
recommended by paid-to-recommend-them journalists:
those of the Daily Hate Fail or other insignificant
sources of alternative bog-roll

My face reflects a gaunt disaffection through the mirrored
window.

Maybe I do need to eat more red meat?

Characterless traits and tropes battle for a broken
home
through a sleeping man's headphones

The Kings of Leon?
More like the kings of predictability!

Ringtone's turned up too high, buzz with pride!
Conversations of bonuses spewed so *laugh-out-loud*.

> We arrive at the next stop; kids play modern-day
> hopscotch around bags on platforms.

I'm a mere ten minutes into the journey and I'm two bottles down
    already; this should ensure my table stays quiet.
> My good lady claims I have a problem with drink!
> The only problem I have with it is the bloody price
> these days!

City lights flash and blur, cursing dark fields of natural habitat –
cows are annulled by the flashing neon lights of capitalist slogans.

> Next stop – the young boy asks his mummy, *Can I
> press the door, please?* She crudely replies, *Of course
> you can, as long as you open it!*

I often wonder why I write notes on such banal non-events.
But I guess an observer will always find something, even in
    nothing!
Plus – the notepad is the perfect distraction; nobody suspects me!

> A peeved looking poncy business twat checks his
> ticket and sees that I'm sat in his seat.
> He dumps his iPad and iPhone on the table, then
> rushes off to find the ticket-checker.
> He could have just asked nicely?

Unfortunately for him it's my stop (I always exit seat last minute).
I pull up my hood and open my bag, take a quick glance around
    for unwanted eyewitness potential.
> The coast is clear, so I liberate his goods, exit train r
> ight and head up the escalator. Not a bad day's work;
> the twat even left the headphones – genuine Apple
> ones too!
> What a swipe!
> I knew this pen and paper would make the
> perfect disguise!

MOTORWAY MASTERPIECES

Just Vape Street
Go Home
Conifer vs Verbena
Lights & ANPR
Phone boxes for emergencies only
Bridges sprayed with treason
(Which I adore)
White arrows –
                    Constantly ignored
Three lanes
              Become one!
Bales of hay
          On a sea of green sidewalk
Signs
Signs
And more signs

Evidence of sin

A stuffed elephant –
Oil-stained

Roads lit-dim

WALK-IN WARDROBE

Last night one of the regulars, Pete Pool Table, informed me of
    his ability to conjure up
a *mean* black-pepper sauce.
So mean, in fact,
that he'd have to kill himself
if he told me.
Either that or kill me
(but he likes me too much to kill me).
It was meant as a compliment... I think?

Today I put it to the rest of the punters:
a response of shrugged shoulders mostly.
Man talks shite!
says Window-view Robbie.

Slot-machine Sammy
jolts his eyes from the flashing lights:
*Now I can't say nowt about the man's cookin', but ah've seen
    his walk-in wardrobe!*

Ooh-ah? I've heard he's handy with the woodwork!
I say, hoping to inspire some more insight.

*Oh aye, lad, his walk-in wardrobe's so handy – that you have to
    get on your hands and knees to crawl through the fucker!
    Ask the man about his crawl-in wardrobe!*

The cacophony of laughter answers my question regarding
    Pete's black-pepper sauce.

#CLOCKS

Time
Is an amputated hand
Clicking its fingers
Keeping rhythm with the dead

WHEN THE SHUTTERS CAME DOWN

I know from the smell/that it's over/taken/
raw placenta hung like fairy lights/
around the chimney breast/open fire/
spit and crackle forms/
from her eyes' waterfall/
blood-orange glint/unwashed hair/
sprayed out like willow bracken/
death-stare/saluted by puff of fag/
ash emptied into warmed Carling can/
You OK?/asked/answer known/
I'm sorry, I mean…/
fingers jam shut lips/
like the shutters of a nightclub at 4am/
no matter what is said/
it's insignificant right now/
the bell has already rung out for last orders

BLESSED

they said he was cursed
bruised fruit
unripe
exiled from his orchard

hacked from the umbilical cord
aborted from the cervix

the regulars called him *Feral Frank*
the lone-wolf lost from the pack
Mr Ne'er-do-well

seated at the end of the bar
watchin' the fruit machine
glass always half-empty

one Friday night
he screamed so loud
that he had a heart attack
having learned
he'd just won the lottery

as the ambulance took him away
the regulars said he was blessed
oh   so   blessed

#ELBOW INTERROGATION

you stare at your elbows in the mirror
red psoriasis itch
never inherited

your elbows ask you
why have we kipped in so many unfamiliar places?

you
look
down

check the room for witnesses

turn your back

evade the mirror

you don't have time for awkward questions

WEEKEND LENS

this ground belongs to me
public space ain't never shared, only portioned
enough guilt lies in wait to be extorted
where pilgrims march beggars tighten tourniquets
ownership ain't a thing in a rat-race
fag-nub city
beggin' for change outside the chippy
every idiot lookin' for a village struts past
stinkin' of Boots aftershave samples that they've blagged
orange men and women doused in fake tan
bouncers, bulldog-necked and pumped up with stedz
posture for position on town's swankiest stretch

MANDEM DRIVE LIKE PRICK AND PRANG OUT THE LOCALS

on park pushing my yoot on swings
when we hears bang like volcano

don't think we got none of them
in the Midlands, let alone Derby

wasteman sprints onto park
followed by fed hot onniz Reeboks

GET DAAHRN YER BASTERD!

gripped up: arms behind back
face to floor: gravel on the tongue

wasteman's soon read his rights
pulled tooiz feet – straitjacketed by handcuffs

holding yoot tight I walk through the gates
back onter street to investigate

five cop cars
two riot vans

jus' pas' ma yard there's a smoked Corsa
invading the wall of the lettin' agents

mashed up an eighteen-plate Audi en route too

as wasteman's shoved into meat wagon
i tellim eezer prick: *that coulda took me
and ma yoot out the game, blud*

responds: *I know, sorry, mate!*

commotion continues
wasteman's accomplice causin' more fuss

I spy my man from up street
lean out his bedroom window

eyes popping from his bludclart skull
like footballs that damn don't fit there

he dashes back in
fed don't seeim

luckily for him it's only man like me
with eyes like a detective on this street

why man so prang, you ask?
well, wouldn't you be?
if this all cracked off outside
when you had a house fulla *grass*?

JESSICA

Shrivelled skin
in an incubator.
Our world.
My saviour.

SOUND CLASH

In the boozer tonight
the landlord's managed
to double-book
the pool team
with the open-mic night.

Now, the pool team
take their pool
very seriously,
so it's fair to say
that they're
none too taken
when the host
approaches them with a request:

Listen, lads, can you turn that fuckin' pool down?
I'm tryin' to wreck a ballad over here!

DELUGE

Deluge waits for her next victim,
harbours fragmented glass, syringe drivers
hepatitis-ridden; heretic fallout from the clear-up
forgotten by the clipboard.

Deluge, hunched, swamped
in diarrhoea-brown puddle,
finds amphibian form,
expands territory with
every knot of wind.

Deluge stares through Pepsi-can eyes,
winks, mocks an abandoned Coca-Cola bottle.

Her Venetian-blind tail curls with caution,
guts rumble; nuts, bolts and lost keys;
attempted growl, but her jaw is clamped shut,
handcuffed by a plastic beer-can holder.

#STREETS

these streets are as quiet
as an England match at Wembley
the boozers are the polar opposite

OUR MAN

FIREWORKS #1

Down at his pappu's old allotment
our man
is warming his hands over the barrel;
a Pikachu mask, along with his clothing, simmers ablaze,
charring into a distant memory.
He slings a penknife like a discus
towards the nearby brook,
feels sentimental, ignores attachment,
listens for the plop,
pulls the pouch of bacca
from his gardening dungarees,
steps down on a woodlouse
with his wellington boots.

ACT 1: THE PURGE

You drink to forget that he's gone.
You drink to forget that your friend is gone.
You drink to forget that he's gone.
You drink to forget that your best friend's gone.

My head's a bag of sweaty Skittles,
colourful thought bubbles
squashed together.
The lump in my throat's getting larger,
a wasp's-nest gasp for breath
before I neck down half a pint in one swig.
A roomful of friends
can soon feel like strangers.
I open my palm to accept his paw
like I did this morning
for the last time at the vet's,
the muzzle
clenched tight around his mouth,
anaconda-tight,
the look in his eyes: confusion,
then out; sparko!
Like Wayne Rooney
at the hands of Phil Bardsley,
except peaceful: void of pain.
At least that's what I convince myself.
The reality is: I feel like a murderer.
I've had to cry; cry away the pain.
The vet left me to hug his body for a while.
He was a big lad: nine-stone American bulldog.
Went by the name of Chops.
A sterling, handsome, loyal dog.
I paid extra dosh
to ensure I get his ashes in a box,
otherwise
they just pile
all the dead dogs' bodies together
and do a communal burning.
Some dignified ending, that.

The same rules apply
if you're lucky enough
to have a state-funded pauper's funeral.
My mate even alleges
that they don't even burn you
in the budget-price wicker basket;
they just toss your body in.
Same outcome, you see,
man or dog,
woman or dog,
non-binary or dog.

And I'll miss the feeling of waking
hazy-eyed with a bladder full of ale
to a dog-breathed lick
as I lie foetal-positioned on the carpet.
I'll miss it all; loved him from pup 'til now.
He was better than people.

See, the problem is
I don't really make much time
for this emotional business.
My job gets in the way
of processing my misery,
cramped up like a hen
in a grey-walled factory.
That's why I end up here,
in the same old spot, night by night,
spitting grief and slicing tongues.
I'm always right and everyone else is wrong,
and I'll stare and I'll frown
and I'll hurl abuse
and the regulars'll say nowt
'cause they know I'm well loose
and they don't wanna see me enter
true beast mode.
So after last orders when everyone goes
I'll still be sat here downing a Stones
until the landlord finally shouts up,
Come on, lad! It's time for you to go!

#IDENTIFYING THE MISSING

The next week at work is character-building.
Hell transcends its vice
upon the office environment.
There's simply no advantage to be gained
from conducing oneself to such a state
at the weekend.
I think deeply about this for a second,
then deeply about a few pints after work,
down the Bird with the lads
in their paint and plastered Snickers trousers.
How I miss that life.
Proper work.
Not like this office malarkey.
Hopefully Sammy (the new barmaid)
would be working the boozer too:
liven the place up a bit!

I consider the truth.
What is the truth?
The *truth* is that I bloody hate work:
the new suited-and-booted career,
the nine-to-five,
everyone I work with.
They're all backstabbers and charlatans,
tossing it off and keeping up appearances.
I hate their mindsets,
their ultra-competitive neoliberal mindsets.
I blame that twat David Cameron.
Danny Dyer was spot on there.
No one can argue with salient facts!
Poor old Dickensian Dave
and his be more *competitive* nonsense.
Be more competitive?
That's why he bloody quit
when he lost his referendum!
Pure hypocrisy, just like the workplace
and the colleagues.
I hate the lot of them.

I hate the arse-licking, the lies,
the backstabbing, the chat-blagging,
the deceit, the emails, the bloody emails!
The notifications; the absence of meaning!
I hate it all.
I hate a lot.
But mostly I just miss:
I miss feeling positive about anything.
I miss the dog-walks.
I miss the dog.
I miss the walks.
I miss myself.

My nemesis *anxiety*
is running laps around my body;
trickles of sweat
race
from the starting line of my neck
to the finish line of my lower back.
A change of atmosphere is apparent.
We are now flying
at an altitude of 99,000 feet
and we don't like it.
The sniggers and fixed stares are palpable.
My colleagues are up to something,
trying to set me loose
even though they know I have it in me
to spit, cackle, howl at the moon
and stab them all with a blunt spoon!
So why choose me?
Is this personal?
A class war?
A vendetta?

I close down my computer
and get up from my chair.
No one stares me directly in the face:
a sure sign that conceit is being dealt.
I head upstairs to the bogs

for a Richard third.
I decide to *crack one off*
on work's time whilst I'm up here!
Forget them; I'm getting paid to wank.
Who are the real fools then?
I focus on my fantasy, depart the real world.

Once returned from my state of deviance
I stand at the mirror,
face my reflection.
Anxiety floods my blood.
MUST KEEP CALM.
I wash, scrubbing my hands and nails
in time to the staccato rhythms
accentuated by my heartbeat.
Pandemonium is on the horizon;
I know her well.
I recognise her embrace and caress,
her power to seduce me into fortitude;
maybe not the right kind of fortitude,
but these pricks
are in need of witnessing something!
Truth is they ain't been dragged up like me.
They're all 2.4 family show homes
and personalised reg plates,
all armed with the cocksure self-assurance
that comes along with knowing
you've a fat inheritance on the horizon!
That comes with knowing
that no matter where
the austerity hammer lands,
you won't be affected.
The truth will always manifest;
the colleagues epitomise this.
There will always be a divide here!
Lines are now drawn.
I steady my breathing
and take the long walk
back downstairs.

When I enter the office
there are more conspicuous stares
and whispers.
When I approach my desk
there's a new screensaver
to greet my return:
one enough to break any Rams fan,
let alone a grieving Rams fan.
There he is: *Chops*, my dead dog,
now wearing a Forest kit.
Some *clever* bastard
has Photoshopped it
onto his poor cancer-ridden body
The picture is recent as well;
the pricks
must've been stalking my Facebook page.
Some motherfucker
thinks they're a proper *Billy Big-Cock*, aye?
The time   for calm   has passed;
it's time to let myself go:
to the freedom of pandemonium!
I flip over the desk,
smash the computer screen.
I pick it up, throw it
in the direction of the gossiping bastards.
I'm spitting with rage
as I charge headfirst at my colleagues
like a bull, bursting with liberation.
It feels so good
and no fucker is coming near us!
I stand amongst my audience and let rip:
> *WHO FUCKIN' WANTS IT, THEN? COME ON, YER WEAK*
> *BASTARDS!*
> *YER AIN'T LAUGHIN' NOW, ARE YER?*
I'm disappointed
by the lack of enthusiasm
on the part of my audience.
I really expected more engagement,

more participation.
I fix them all with dead eyes
as I storm out of the office
like a gale-force wind.
THE   GAME IS   UP!

When I reach reception
Dave or Charles
or whatever the fuck his name is
implores me to sign out!
Luckily for him my knuckles are bleeding.
The discomfort
on the wanker's face is encouraging;
I sign my name in blood.
The next week at work is definitely
my last week at work.

OUR MAN

I

Our man
has fled the page of hegemony,
war-torn and bleedin' detachment.
Our man,
first in the pub,
last to leave.
Our man,
from fit fiddle to organ rupture,
from solid joiner to rickety structure.
Our man
omits signals from deluded stations,
engages in the refusal of social invitations.
Our man
ain't just stayin' off the drugs;
he's stayin' off the people!
Our man,
only halfway through his life,
is already focused on the sequel.
Our man
has signed an abatement order
against his soul,
mind plagued   neurons severed,
is on the verge of himself   lamented by absence.
Our man,
the voice of treason   hammer to the nail.
Our man
has walked out on himself.

II

Our man
is lost to the conflicted voices in his skull;
backed against the wall, can he even stand tall?
Our man
can remove his masks and face his reflection.
Our man
ain't as doomed as he believes,
may well question what he achieves.
Our man
needs to nurture his self-belief.
Our man
is a part of us all.
Hold him up.
Don't let him   fall.

#OUR BOY

Our boy's sixteen
when his mam beats the drum;
her time raising him's done.
Nah, yer out on yer own, son.
She's got crack habit *ter manage,*
so it's time fer him *ter get gone!*

Our boy asks his local council for support;
it don't arrive.
He gets lost in the system like he never existed,
sleeps it rough,
starts on the *spice of life* diet,
mambulance on constant standby.

Our boy
soon adjusts to his climate without complaint.

Three weeks later
he begs up the dollar to buy a tent.
Our boy sets it up on a waste ground
he knows don't command no rent.
In the middle of the night, he gets firebombed –
straight-up firebombed! –
by some *yocal bludclart,*
who assumes
the tent's housing *asylum seekers*:
> GET AAART MAH FUCKIN' COUNTRY, YER ISLAMIST
> SCUMBAGS!
> THIS IS MAAAAH FUCKIN' ENGLAND, NOT YOURS!

When our boy rushes out stun-faced
the *yocal* bludclart looks terrified,
starts stampin' the fire out with his feet,
but the tent's mashed-up
and our boy's beyond strapped for cash.
Yocal bludclart offers him a settee at his yard; *it's the least he
can do.*

The next day *yocal* bludclart
finds himself homeless
with a mashed-up face;
it was the least our boy could do!

DAVEY #1

Cousin Davey

writes from pen.

Sezziz clean now; bin sixteen months.

I want to believe him... but
even if it's true
I'll give him sixteen minutes once he's out here.

It's got nowt to do with availability;
there's nuff drugs in there!

It's down to influence.
Cousin Davey's got plenty wrong ones
followin' him round
like an underworld chemical cloud
rainin' uppers and downers.

OUR MAN AT THE THEATRE

With the pub as his theatre
our man enters stage left.
This ain't no cameo appearance.
Cantankerous comments
fire from haggard old mouths
amidst the chaos
of Saturday-afternoon lager louts'
bullet-dashed verbal blasts,
inept to our man right now;
volume's muted on the lot of 'em!

Tuned in to a game of Countdown in his head.
He's on the final round right now:
the conundrum.
The word's obvious but he can't see it,
shouts and spits at the telly.

Man United are on,
so no one thinks nowt of it
Our man hates the red devils
as much as he hates the red dogs.
Shouting is standard procedure for him, really.

A-B-U![1]
Ronnie shouts over,
raising a Carling pot in his direction.

Our man
does not compute; he's a fade in the distance, departed and
delirious

Sammy asks him how he is.
He wants to tell her,
wants to tell them all
how   he   is,
really, he does,

_____

1 Anyone but United

47

but he doesn't;
he doesn't tell them nowt.
Not about her,
not about him,
not about this,
not about that,
not about missing the fucking dog,
not about missing the fucking kid.

Words
are an incomplete formation
using his tongue as a trampoline,
rotting
like a dead carcass in his head.

OUR MAN'S PRIDE 'N' THAT...

The memories   fragmented,
squashed,
jarred,
derelict,
like the instacoffee
heaped into his perma-tanned cup,
kettle flicked on but lightless,
switch pressed down
repeatedly with venom
like you do
the broken stapler you need to work.
Plug's out   no idea why.
Checks the lecky meter; void of juice.
These tossers are so thirsty these days.

His soul's
the repossessed house
in your neighbourhood,
the one boarded up,
ransacked for scrap metal and wire.
His heart pumps forlorn adrenaline;
prospects of leaving his abode
mutilate his mind.

Spat out onto the street
like hangover phlegm,
cohesive glands tense,
reticent whispers invade his ears,
stars aligned
with no purpose.

Glances the reflection in the car window,
vision set to peripheral/arbitrary;
reheated matter slops through his veins,
scarred knuckles boiled to the brim,
accustomed to insignificance,
no last rites of passage.

Bashes into a blue bin; contagion.
Recycling day was last bloody week.
An invader
is not an invader if they are ever-present,
a subliminal carrot dangled,
smack to a junky.
The cup's half-empty
and there's no room for dunking;
the purpose of the plot is to lose it!
That's what they tell him;
that's what he already knows,
but the confirmation is appreciated.

Our man's an absconder
let loose in the grounds of purgatory,
no time for backtracking,
hackles stretched and growling;
in his feet cultures clash,
his identity a distant echo under a rainbow.

Full-moon Monday; no work done,
one helluva task,
solid stature maintained
as he walks past the old workplace,
spots former colleagues
through dislocated blinds,
a bottle of champers in the office after shift,
mind bubbling a broth of negativity.
The culprits are everywhere:
slogans and lies dressed as statistics.

Our man penetrates the shop for lecky,
needs fags 'n' all.

stutter
stutter
stutter
Yes, sir?
stutter
stutter
stutter

Stop; breathing apparatus activated!
Ten Embassy Number 1, ta, duck!
Confusion slaps the shopkeeper's face.
We only sell them in twenties now, sir; we stopped selling ten-
    decks months ago!
Sniggers,
smooched teeth
and the waft of noses
emanate from the queue
that's formed behind him.

Our man turns round
to glare yoots; staring machetes,
his eyes exit screwface glare,
pupils diverted to the floor,
refocused on the till.
Bocker
is muttered under the shopkeeper's breath,
as casual as a compliment.
Our man pretends not to hear it.
No tens? Bloody 'ell; twenty, then, twenty Embassy Number 1!
He squares up the bill, leaves the shop.

He feels deconstructed
like a Meccano play set,
one that'll never be used again.

You will never know our man
until you discover
the depths of his pride.

LOVE

Sammy the barmaid averts her eyes
from the pint of Foster's she's pouring.
Drips attack the floor.

Our man tracks her gaze
like a football copper scanning faces
for banned DLF members at Pride Park stadium.
He zooms in through her retinae,
watches her *watching Love*
as Love
heads to the bogs
for a piss and a sniff.

FIREWORKS #2

Our man's thin sleep is unveiled;
familiar thunder of fireworks
reverberates the terraced streets
with shotgun ricochet.

Next-door's baby cries
louder than Jesus Christ.
At the third stroke
the time is 3.03am.

Riled instantaneously upright
he preps agile attire,
clobber he wears for dog-walks:
joggers, hood, balaclava, gloves

Out the back door,
fence-hopping,
interrogates smoke,
determines origins.

Another rocket is unleashed
in synchronicity with a door slammed shut on giggling RP voices;
their audacity is simply untenable.

David Attenborough's vocal style
rushes through his head:

Unlike the urban mandem,
the middle-to-upper-clarse student
is not naturally equipped with the feral capabilities required
in order to best survive the harsh urban environments of
the Midlands.

Our man ponders:
what fronts such cockiness?
He grills this notion
like a philosophical enquiry.
Initial analysis leads him

to the field of *martial arts*.
He'd be willing to bet his possessions
one of these pricks was at least first dan.

The trouble with martial arts is
its reliance upon idealised scenarios.
Dreams were not prevalent around here.
The best martial artists he knew
were street-fighters.
Being privileged
and professionally trained
didn't count for much in his book,
not in a dark terraced-house garden;
execution required restraint.

The focus here was inebriation
and showing off to yer mates.
Everybody's skin was the same:
thin beneath the pressure of a blade.

Our man focuses,
thoughts erupt his subconscious,
the *god* of the working classes had spoken,
our man merely conduit.

The words race through his mind
like Usain Bolt at the London Olympics,
digested like the inauguration speech
of an *actually* decent politician.

Fornicated Fanta cans, pin-pricked,
torn tongues from crack-pipe inhalation,
messages transmitted on strings:
makeshift telephone exchange.

Tasting the blood on his tongue,
sedated by the antivenom,
enough to nullify any class structure,
he hops three more gardens.

On a trampoline he spots a Pikachu mask.

SATURDAY MORNING/SUNDAY MOURNING

Blue Mattress Hotel,
as hostile as ever;

no idea why he's here.
Recalls a Jägerbomb breakfast,
Forest away at the City ground,
beating them with ten men,
some shit with a bouncer;
ah, figures.

Our man needs a shit:

no bog roll.

Our man's on the buzzer at the double

(he takes a wank under the brown sheets whilst he waits).

When the hatch opens
he grabs the tracing-paper-thin bog roll
from the copper; spunk slopped in his palms,
the copper's face is a Picasso painting
as our man's spunk finds a new home
on the back of his hand.

Our man shits
for England, Cyprus, Wales, Ireland,
and every other country in his genetic makeup he is yet to
discover,

refuses the breakfast,
would rather contract hepatitis.

DAVEY #2

Cousin Davey writes again,
sezziz bin stabbed twice in the face
by a *cuppla Lesta man.*
Sezzy teefed-up some shotter
who was in there *tinkin iz bad*;
shotter couldn't strut his stuff though,
gevvit the big guns but weren't *ruff* enough,
shotter put a hit out on Cousin Davey's head.

Cousin Davey
sezzy wrestled *both man off*,
but they stabbed 'im up iniz face in the fracas.

Cousin Davey got hospitalised, shipped off the block;
he'll be moved *onter nex jail* when he gets out.
Cousin Davey *sez* dunt write him back again jus yet
cuzzy dunt know where he'll be *settlin'.*

Cousin Davey's face
must be a fuckin' mess!

OUR MAN THE DESTITUTE SOLDIER

Our man's keys are destitute,
a jingly mass of homeless dross;
they've been sold out,
replaced, de-barrelled,
exiled from the locks.

Our man's shoes don't fit;
they never did,
soles invalid, bereft of guilt,
fabric stained from liquors spilt.
They've walked too many dive bar floors,
hunted the dodgiest streets for scores.

Our man's jeans
are knackered too,
torn down the crotch
at a Northern soul do
attempting the splits
like a failed Agadoo.

Our man's shirt
rides up at the waist.
He used to have a six-pack;
now he's carrying a crate
of jellied flesh, wobbling on a plate.

Take the piss all you like,
'cause our man
really
couldn't give a crap,
'cause appearances mean nowt
to his baseball bat.

OUR MAN IN THE COLISEUM

grief   disembowels   neurons
logical clause invalidated
sympathy   concern   empathy
deflected with equal disdain
apathy the age-old sin
manufactures mutations
cracked scar tissue
disingenuous   plagued   egos
our   man a mere   spectator
in a blood-lusting coliseum of business-speak wolves
snarl   flesh   hackles raised like champagne flutes

a chimney stack on the horizon
    pockmarked with melted plastic
facilitates toxic smoke
    as the guests admire the view
prawn sandwiches on tap   bubbles   wine   cheesecake
    our man is soon down on all fours
foaming   hacking   kickback   from   the
ticker
the cheesecake not the gerbils   for dog's sake not the gerbils
his colleagues now incandescent with pride
as the ambulance arrives
paramedics trawl the stairs
once resuscitated
his colleagues line up for selfies
next to the stretcher

OUR MAN'S MA

Despite being thirty-five years old
our man still finds himself in pubs,

threatening to slice up his mates and
burn down their houses for
trying it on
with his ma.

Our man ain't so sure he'll ever
outgrow this kind of behaviour.

Our man might be reformed
but he'll never   be *that*   reformed.

LUCY

Our man
sees his childhood sweetheart, *Lucy*, in town,

witnesses her perform a casual waltz
through the doors of Boots.
Security alarm bleeds out.
Some lad in a stained Adidas tracky top
legs it past her;
overweight security guards chase in pursuit.

Our man knows that Lucy's got the goods;
leg-it stained tracky is just a mere decoy.

Our man looks Lucy straight in the eyes.
Jeez, she's changed; he ain't seen her for time.

Lucy stares through his eyes,
glazed with disdain
as though
he was the open hatch
to a paedophile's prison cell.

In this moment
our man feels as numb
as Lucy's soul,
numb
as the paedophile's cell door.

#NUB

Our man bustles past
puddles of
blood and sick on Wardwick,
alky haze
phenomenon,
glazed-over eyes
like a stained-glass finish,
stomach lined
with a shoal of darting swordfish;
they breaststroke through his kidneys.

Flesh-tunnelled ears
flap like flags in the wind.

He itches tics like Tourette's,
tunes in to the chorus of
OI, MY SHIT'Z BIN TUK, YER BASTERDS!
Nobody sees him do it.

Our man's now walking backwards,
kerb-crawling,
his own shadow
scouring tarmac
for fag nubs,
enough bacca for a joint.

MORE OR LESS

they couldn't afford the honeymoon period
they did without
drifted through the waves of matrimony
one a man of bottled-up messages
in a bottle full of whiskey
words of firewater leaking out
indecipherable to any reader
nightmarish for any listener

our man cast out to ride the seas
of the gutters

once aboard the raft of Stella cans
the lifetime Aldi carrier bag
is called into action
hoisted into a new life
as a makeshift flag

he embraces the wind
swaying his head
nodding like a buoy in his own polluted sea
wetness of cheek is ignored
drip-down waterfall
salted tongue

clarity cognates
eventually   when love supplies are low
admittedly
he could definitely give her more
but that didn't mean   that he required less

#MAN DOWN

Our man's down,
floor-bound,
no stabilisers,
dint need 'em.

Our man's lying on his back,
tarmac used like hammock,
sunshine of February
reimagined as July Aleppo.

Coordination of reality
unattempted,
public shoes patter pavements like paratroopers
marching through imperial streets.

Our man lacks the nowse to converse,
chapped lips impoverished.
There is a sign next to him:
CLEANING IN PROGRESS,
cleans his soul
with the soles of his feet.

Spots a Tic Tac amongst the fag nubs,
mouth open and willing,
bites down.

Sober as a judge but high as a kite, guvnor!
Yer holding up three fingers, you pillock!
Yes, I'm quite aware this is the floor!
I'm also aware of my right to be here!

Our man's down and talking to the wind;
it responds to him only.

Beguiled by nature's caress,
our man reaches for a crisp packet: prawn cocktail,
thrown away in repellence,

wind taken by the scruff of neck,
snot dripping to the lips,
clinging
for dear life.

RAIL TRACKS

Our man was found
down by the rail tracks
behind his old flat on the estate,
not dead or nowt,
just chillin' on the grass with a can of Coke.

He looked disturbed,
disturbed
'cause they'd disturbed him,
and they were right to conclude
that he appeared that way
'cause they'd disturbed him.

If they hadn't
then he wouldn't look disturbed.

Until they'd arrived
he'd looked as chuffed as
a young lad watching
Thomas the Tank Engine
for the first time

He wished
they'd just
fuck off.
He'd not come here to see them

DRUG DEAL VOYEURISM

departs the Merc 4x4
eyes like a pedestrian crossing
carrier bag, bulbous, abounds with goods
whiff stronger than a spliff
whizzes to hit nostril hairs that stiffen
his face is pranger
than the definition of prang
I've never seen so much sweat hang from man
he looks around
what for?
only he knows
if it's CID?
well, he ain't gonna see those
he marches the cobblestones
quick-time on his toes
with his carrier bag full of skunk
blissfully unaware
that he's made it into this book

OUR MAN OF EFFICACY

Our man
robbed Peter to pay Paul but paid no one.
Our man
refused to grovel,
fessed up that he'd messed up.
Got carried away on the session,
sniffed the lot.

When the cold lead of gun-butt
fleeced his spine
that January night,
his posture fixed upright
with expectation,
trepidation didn't come into it.

At least one lad behind,
two more before his eyes,
balaclavaed up.
Back doors
swung open on the Transit,
flapped like an eagle's wingspan.

Our man just stepped in,
smiled,
gold tooth glistening in the streetlight,
for he knew

that he was far too useful

                    to kill.

GIVE 'EM THE ROPE

there was this helpline
he'd call it daily
at first there were operators
nice lads and lasses

then the funding got cut
so he just rang a dead line
let it ring through
to the answer machine
they'd forgotten to switch off
it was handy they'd forgotten
as it meant
he could bench-press the atlas
off of his chest

one not very fine Sunday
the number rang dead
as in *dead*
that long depressed monotone drone

this number was not available
but this number
was the only one he could speak to
some form of emotional algebra he'd deciphered
the number got his spirits high
its formation always appealed
simply for the number of sevens contained within its makeup

even if it only rang
never answered
even if the inbox was full
never emptied
he'd talk and sing away
bladdered from the boozer

but
    not
        if
          it
             was
                dead

he had this problem with reality
they'd fallen out
no longer mates
barely even acquainted by now

when he didn't show up for work
no one thought nowt of it –
probably bin sessioning again
the daft twat

locally
there was this politician
who'd signed off the paperwork to cut the funds for the helpline
a few days later
this politician complained to his chauffeur about the traffic
whilst a soon-to-be-traumatised
young copper
kicked off a front door
after numerous failed chaps at the letterbox

PLACING WAGERS

The pub had started taking bets on our man,
when he'd break for proper,
what he'd do,
how long he'd get.
Foregone conclusions were predicted.

When our man lost his shit,
he   lost   his   shit!

Our man heard about the wagers,
encountered the idle chat
through Chinese whispers,
understood that they were too stupid,
too stupid to see
how lucky they were
not to lose their lives.

In his youth
idle chat would've cost them just that.

You could take a life physically,
but that was a bit bait these days,
hard to get away with,
messy.

Psychological warfare, on the other hand,
could be deployed discreetly
if you possessed the necessary skills.
Our man was a man possessed,

but for now he'd keep his ear to the ground.
Whichever cunt won the dosh
owed him more than just a pint;
he'd see to that.

No matter what he did and how long he got
when shit hit the fan,
come release day
this place'd be his first port of call.

#BLACKEYED ON CHRISTMAS EVE

Our man
is black-eyed and walkin' round
like everyone done it.
Who it was?
Ask the night,
ask the pigeon-shit cobbled streets,
ask the takeaway,
the taxi driver,
the half-gnawed kebab.
Our man
thinks everyone done it,
eveeeeerrrrryyyyy-ooooonnneeee!
Our man has tinsel in his eyes,
mince pies in his nostrils.
Our man is on a stare-out frenzy,
enjoys the looks of confusion
penned across the chops
of people out
on their last-minute Christmas shops.
Blokes with tattoos on their necks are best
'cause blokes with tattoos on their necks
always give you dirty looks
for staring at the tattoos on their necks.
Our man loves it,
loves it better than best,
feels like shouting aloud,
You ought to have seen the other geezer!
You ought to have fuckin' seen him!
when the truth is
our man
didn't even see him.Cobwebs

the cobwebs mask the cracked ceiling
dim the strip-light invasion
surround the seat-less metal toilet
like Christmas tinsel round the fireplace
our man reaches for the buzzer
the cobwebs christen his eyes like sleep-dust

the hatch opens to a polystyrene cup
he drinks the dry water
tastes the cobwebs on his tongue like popping candy
his breath is squashed to a pulp
by the arachnoid children born of his gullet
they swarm his glands   claim the space
of his extradited tonsils

he hums the nursery rhyme 'Itsy Bitsy Spider'
reaching for the buzzer once more he hangs in the air like a
moth
flapping under the light; entrenched in the cobwebs of his
mind
he'll never   be free again

cobwebs bleed out from the floor
scale his legs   melt his limbs
to the crescendo of an unfixed junky
screaming from the Blue Mattress Hotel next door

light escapes from a chip in the glass
the only speck they forgot to mask
cobwebs entangle his eyes
like he's wearing cobwebbed contact lenses

he needs a fag
there's the bacca, Rizla, and two matches stashed down his
pants

he reaches into his darkest region
produces a long thread of cobweb
that the paraphernalia
have attached themselves to
he rolls with sweaty Rizla
and smokes...

the copper is soon back at the hatch
our man just exhales in his face and laughs
laughs
laughs

come on, lad, you know you can't do that
how on earth did you sneak it all in here anyway, man?

no strip-search, duck! and where I'm headed the rulebook's
  out the window, brother!

the hatch slams shut and nowt more is said about it

the cobwebs weave him to sleep standing up
a pretty comfortable one too, considering the circumstances

THE RAIN

our man
cruises the boozers in town
like a loyal barfly
finds shelter
under a Foster's umbrella
in a beer garden

some young lad
surrounded by gyaldem
starts givin' it the bazza

(Derby slang for
givin' it the big 'un
as in
givin' it the Bazza
as in
givin' it the Barry McGuigan:
the big 'un)

all our man can remember
is glass dancing in the rain

colliding
with flesh
at the speed
of a train

followed by a thunderstorm of blood

blood

more blood

INTERGALACTIC SEXUAL RELATIONS?

Our man wakes up on the settee,
brand new Fred Perry,
covered in brown fluff.
In the mirror
he looks
like he's been shagging Chewbacca.

FIREWORKS #3

A male student with a stitched-up, slash-marked face is talking to a policeman in a dirty kitchen...

So let me get this straight... you were setting off fireworks at three in the morning?

Y-y-yes, officer.

OK, and then a man in a Pokey-mon mask appeared in your garden, slashed you across the face with some sort of knife, and then ran off down the entry?

Y-y-yes, officer, it was a Pikachu mask, and before I knew it he was gone in a flash, like a bad dream or something!

I thought you said it was a Pokey-mon mask? I'm finding this incident confusing enough to process without you changing the details, so was it a Pokey-mon mask or a Chikkachu mask or whatever it is you just said?

Pikachu is a type of Pokémon, officer; you know, that cute little yellow one you've probably seen about?

I can assure you that I don't see many Pokey-mon about on this job, lad, but thanks for clarifying this. I guess I've got all I need, and the lads from forensics have already been out, right?

Y-yes, they came more or less immediately. Well, so I'm told; obviously I was in the ambulance on the way to hospital.

Well, that's good, then; hopefully they've found something that'll help us with our enquiries. We're already out going door-to-door as we speak. Do try and think if there's anybody you've upset though, won't you? I mean, aside from every street within half a mile!

So do you, you know, think you'll catch him?

I always say in these cases that they'll normally end up catching themselves, bragging about it down the pub or something. Unless it's a professional, in which case it could prove more problematic...

What do you mean by a professional? Should I still be worried? I mean, will I get some kind of protection?

I suspect that as long as you don't go letting off any more fireworks at three in the morning you'll be just fine, lad. Maybe think about that in future; you students aren't too popular with the locals round here as it is. This crime bears all the ingredients of a hacked-off neighbour, but, seeing as you didn't see where they went and we've found no weapon or cute yellow Pokey-mon mask, as you put it, it's hard to tell. Anyway, I'll be on my way. You've got our number if there's anything else that springs to mind.

Mm, okay, er, yeah, thanks for your help... I guess.

As the copper gets back into his car he realises he's deleted the majority of the statement. He taps it into the device again, but he can't remember what the bloody Pokey-mon was called. Forget it, he thinks; he's not going in to talk to that snooty little melt again. He hates student houses; in fact, he hates students, full stop.

DOG WALKS

Our man's out walking the dog collar again.
He drags it through the autumn leaves,
manoeuvring past an oil patch.
Come on, boy, there's a good lad.
In the reflection of a car window
he sees Chops:
panting, slobber hanging from his gob.

Stops at the next car,
hides the dog collar
from the little yappers over the road,
doesn't want Chops kicking off,
waking the bloody street up.
Waves at the yappy owner:
Cold morning, aye, duck?
The yappy owner looks across the street
at our man
with his dog lead attached
to an empty collar.
Yappy owner raises his eyebrows,
returns the wave. *Aye, 'tis just that.*
Yappy owner reasons
that grief works in mysterious ways.
Poor bastard, he mutters under his breath
as our man
heads down the street
towards the park.

AFFIRMATION

*

when he discovered his own dereliction
it was welcomed
        by others mainly
but a welcome is a welcome nonetheless

he sipped his last pint
sparked his last spliff
rolled his last note
snorted his last line
queenie winked at him
mocked his wry eyes
tested for water

sustenance was but a word
subtlety an unattainable action

once down
he lay there for days
not because he wanted to
not because of comfort
not because of anything
but because that's all he could do

downstairs he'd hear the punters
as lost as him
but at least they'd found the door
pool balls clash, glasses clink
the slotty drops coins
to fill the till

he considers the chip pan bubbling
from the kitchen
a broth of potato shavings
unloved onion rings
shards of batter

right now
it would make a good hat
this was in fact
the best idea
he'd had for eons

**

the rain drips from the bust gutter outside
were the final straw
to the camel's back
then it was paralysed
nature had lost her charm
he questioned their existence
both nature and charm
both as guilty as a judge

there were other ways
to achieve the possible
he could get hold of a shooter piece of piss
could score one easier than a bag of peng green
different styles too: Uzis, Glocks, shotties, you name 'em
he even met a lad who could get hold of grenades
he had at least three knives'd do the job no bother
but these methods lacked the originality
he wanted out
but not predictability
he considered that a grenade might do the trick
but there was a risk with this methodology
other casualties were a real possibility
imagine if a dog walked past when he did it
that'd be fucked
he went back to the drawing board

***

for a while he just put his pen to the page
let it wiggle in dyslexic scribble
drew heads hanging from nooses
men and women tortured on the cross like Christ (the saviour)
it resembled a new style of hieroglyphics
one the Mayans would be jealous of
he'd watched a documentary on them once
felt he was a throwback
before he knew it
Kurt Cobain graced the page in that stripey jumper he'd
always
    loved
the Dennis the Menace one
he got halfway through writing his suicide note
screwed it up
tossed it in the bin
it was way too predictable

****

it took him another two days of lying down to decipher the
code
he didn't change his boxer shorts in that time
he'd stopped wanking so what was the point?
he thought about snake kings and emperors
the Mayans were into them as well

Stone Fiery Torch
a king's name he'd never forget
remembered it from the documentary
wanted to change his name by deed poll
still fuckin' did

there were snake queens and princesses too
Tikal was the biggest Mayan city
archaeologists were enamoured
by its sophisticated design
the Mayans understood the concept of zero
way before any other society
he wondered if they'd sussed
what less
than that was

*****

on the third day he reached enlightenment
the chip pan was Tikal
the snake emperor told him so last night
the only way to find his heaven
was to embrace it
he couldn't afford
a plane ticket to South America
so the chip pan provided a cheaper alternative
plus the method contained the originality he required
nobody had done this yet
he'd Googled it from three different computers just to be sure
he turned on Tikal at the plug
he then jockeyed the fridge into position covering the door
he necked ten diazepam and five tramadol
began chanting the lyrics he'd memorised from one of the
songs
    of Dzitbalché
an American poet had translated these
original Mayan manuscripts
and he'd found them online

Nuh Shima Ca-la tiki ray
seeki ruh shamina donga tiki ray
Nuh Shima Ca-la tiki ray
seeki ruh shamina donga tiki ray
Ces Shima Ca-la tiki ray
seeki ruh shamina donga tiki ray
Ces Shima Ca-la tiki ray
seeki ruh shamina donga tiki ray

he stripped his clothes
spread them in a circle to symbolise a fire
he took one sock
shoved it as deep into his gullet
as it would go
he peered over Tikal
her fat bubbles hissed at his naked torso; snake gods were

present
the smell of burnt flesh mixed with chip fat
filled his nostrils like eucalyptus
on a really bad day
he prepared
breathing deep
before performing an intense masturbatory ceremony
one for the Mayan gods
one for Stone Fiery Torch, his one remaining guiding light
when his climax peaked
he sprayed his spunk into the chip fat like a porn star
it'd be a shame not to let someone fry chips in it afterwards
it would be a selfish act
but sacrifice came at a cost
as his spunk boiled to a broth
he grabbed the oven gloves
taking her gently he emptied her love
over his head
made his descent toward her core
opening the gates of Mayan Tikal
once inside he met the snake emperor
who provided him
with a harem of snake princesses
his screams were not screams
they were just shouts aimed at a dirty sock
the pain was not pain
it was just his mind deceiving him
his burns were not burns; they were just ungrateful flesh
it just needed cooking through properly
the pain would only subside
once he was well-done
as the diazepam kicked in
he knew
he *knew* he'd reached Tikal
and that Stone Fiery Torch was satisfied

******

he'd cooked himself for around an hour
when the fire alarm finally rang into action
the barmaid Sammy came up from downstairs to see what was
    happening
have you burnt the bloody toast again, duck?
she shouted on her way up the steep flight
she tried the kitchen door
but couldn't move it
a fridge in the way causes that problem
they make good barricades, do fridges
he'd imagined it a stone for his tomb
he'd even stuck his hieroglyphics to it
once he'd gotten them out of the bin
they looked a bit shabby, but fuck it
he was council estate
not fuckin' Buckingham

luckily Big Bryan the bodybuilder was in for his Friday bevs
    downstairs
Sammy ran back down to fetch him
when they returned
Bryan made short work of banging the fridge over
when the door burst open
he wailed, grunted, curled over, puked
the head-rush worse
than his personal best bench press (220 kg)
Sammy thought Bryan was having a seizure
until she saw through his eyes
screaming through salted tears
she ran back down the stairs nearly slipping on a Domino's
pizza flyer
if only she could understand
that she'd just witnessed
the settlement of Tikal
for the first time in Derby

****

his death went down as misadventure
the coroner's verdict
a sexual act
gone wrong...
they just didn't fucking get it, did they?

UNDERDOG CITY

OUR CITY WILL NEVER FORGET

months on
the car-park-cum-shrine
a reminder

your smile
twinkles from
broken glass tarmac

a pelican crossing
now passing place
for doves

these cobbled streets
mourn your departure
angel-faced void

this poet-cum-parent
is convulsed by sand
dashed over fuel spillage

I well up the waterfall
this city needs wept
there's a price on my head

a bounty of words
I cannot find
to convey sympathy

for this meteorite
that entered her family's lives
a meteorite
that time
could never heal

LV TGZ

TREV LVZ TASH
TREVOR LVZ TASHA 016
TRV LVZ TSH
TREVOR LVZ TASHA 4EVA

Now,
I don't know Trevor or Tasha,
but
I can feel their tainted love
insurrected
through these potholed paths
where
their passion is sprayed,
tagged,
for time immemorial.

TREV LVZ TASH
TREVOR LVZ TASHA 016
TRV LVZ TSH
TREVOR LVZ TASHA 4EVA

Discarded beer bottles battle cider cans,
a used Johnny of spent spunk:
Trevor?
I can only guess the guilty deed –
indiscreet,
an old-school Head bag of soiled clothes,
the smashed
box of records: Sham 69, Buzzcocks,
Ramones and the Ruts.

TREV LVZ TASH
TREVOR LVZ TASHA 4EVA

and don't I just know it?

AT ONE WITH NATURE

One night a car was driven onto the field and set alight.
It was extinguished only by a storm; no fire engine was called.
Days turned to weeks – the spoiler fell towards stained grass.
Dogs ran up to the beastly shell, grazing paws on shards of glass.

Weeks turned to months when the local kids utilised the space.
Graffiti appeared, first through rude statements – then a beautiful
    locust,
the inevitable ram, even an elephant; they made the most of the
    canvas,
branding nature upon the shell constructed by man and robot.

When spring arrived dandelions sprouted through the cracks
in the rotted footwells accompanied by verbenas.
One morning I saw an old dear admire them and take photos.
The grass was never trimmed; no one seemed to own the land.

One night I glimpsed a fox's head through the windowless frame.
She appeared to be sheltering her cubs from the incoming rain.
The void space of melted glovebox provided storage for the day's
    forage.
By summer the grass had grown and all but the roof remained
    invisible.

Butterflies and bugs would rest there, providing prey for passing
    birds.
One day at 9am the tow truck eventually arrived to take the shell
    away,
but none of the locals were happy, as it now formed part of the
    landscape.

Plus

they all predicted what came next:

a tarmac car park surrounded by a steel fence.

NOTHING EVER HAPPENS IN DERBY...

There's an anaconda tearing through our city,
slashing through streets like knife through jelly.

It's revealed buried tracks
from our industrial past,

rechristened St Peter's Street
St Mamba's Street,

where beaten brethren congregate
beneath the noses of the CID.

We've people working on the ground
attempting to turn this city around,

but there's just no stopping this anaconda slashing through
our
    city,

leaving survivors frothy-mouthed, eyes back-flipped, jeans
    stonewashed yellow.

We're the Mamba capital of the world!
is the verdict from the hostels, prisons and rehab wards.

There's no constitution for addiction, so there can be no clause
or *indefinite* cause for this affliction,
so where does the contract end?

That unwritten law now Tipp-Exed out:
Those bloody addicts hangin' about.

Like they're enjoying themselves?
Like they're revelling in their opportunity to make a bed in a
    bank doorway?

This anaconda is slashing through our city
like a Hollywood movie,
but I don't think Ice Cube's gonna save us this time.

This anaconda is slashing through our city,

all beneath a sign that reads:

Nothing   Ever   Happens   In Derby

BIN DAY/AUTUMN/TERRACED STREETS

Autumnal leaves battle with crisp packets in the breeze.
The local birds have left their mark on car windscreens.

A session-head, asleep, caresses a cold kebab caked in
grease,
slouched on the corner of the street, unaware he's in his briefs.

The cacophonous rapture of after-sex laughter.
The silhouette of one-night lovers, embraced in satisfaction.

Terraced streets on dustbin day, always junk left on the
footway.
Metal scraps, old bedframes, bin bags and carpets of last year
    remain.

A panic-ridden hedgehog finds a hiding place
from the local tomcats, who spot good game.

A left stiletto, black hairbrush, red leather bag.
A cream, bloodstained jacket, torn into rags.

Footprints on the door, with a smashed windowpane.
My bloody neighbour's left the entry-gate open again!

The taxi driver speeds past, on the graveyard shift,
picking up punters from parties, still half-pissed.

I get back inside the house and loosen the dog's lead.
As some people's days are ending, others just begin.

I boil the kettle and butter the toast, as the central heating
kicks
    in.

WE ARE DERBY

We are Derby.

Rail-track city; birthplace of the industrial revolution,
where inventors span cogs to engineer solutions.

We're a city that delivers,
from Royal Mail PO boxes
to Royal Crown Derby china.
Craft and specialism's our definer.

We are Derby.

Bearers of Joseph Strutt's philanthropy,
Erasmus Darwin's philosophy,
where Florence Nightingale hatched plans
to revolutionise the healthcare of England.

We're engineers with dirty fingernails.
Graft and sweat pump through our veins.
We're Rolls-Royce engines, Belper nails
Toyota motors, Bombardier trains.

We are Derby.

A picture painted by Wright.
A building designed by Pickford.
We're artistic souls and working minds
with a heritage built on cognizance.

The underdog city of middle England,
entrepreneurship exemplified,
where independent businesses thrive;
the real ale capital, a beer festival every night!

We are Derby.

Where the ram is our symbol,
the city its beating heart.
We've lived through hard times, persevered.
Our people possess the spark.

We are Derby County:
formed in 1884,
one hundred years before I was born.
Under Clough and Taylor came the glory days.
The heritage they forged; their legacy still remains.

Where on Shaftesbury Cres the kids now play,
where houses stand and turf once lay
on the ashes of our baseball ground
they laugh and have a kick around.
As Stevie Bloomer watches down
the city's pride emanates the ground.

We are Derby.

On that Monday morning
after that Wanchope weekend
driving all those Man United fans
completely round the bend.

We're resilience in the flesh.
We've never settled
for second-best.
Just walk these streets.
You'll feel the pride.
It's in our DNA.

We are Derby.

Where the future's bright:
bright black and white.

Whoever the opponent,
we'll take the fight.

We'll sing the songs; we'll sing them loud,
whatever gets thrown at us!
The ambition's here, the time is now.
Our loyal supporters will see us proud.
With our new blood we can make the push
and forge new history to elevate this club
back to the top where we belong.
The ambition here is bubbling strong.
We are Derby: Derby County.

SNAKES OF GREED

NINETEEN EIGHTY-FOUR WAS NOT AN INSTRUCTION MANUAL

This was not intended to be an instruction manual,
but you have interpreted it that way.

Subterfuge the souls of cavernous sheeple.
Apply pressure through hateful media.

Fool the commoners.
Engage them with oligarchs dressed like peasants.
Let the hierarchy rise like skyscrapers!
The proletariats will stagnate, naturally,
terrace-housed – hutched in.
When left,
they will peck away at each other like angry, hungry hens.
Not once will they point their beaks towards the farmer.

Crime has risen but fallen by the wayside.
You've got bigger priorities now –
kids to starve, beds to block, speed cameras to clock,
homeless folks to move on to more dereliction –
not to mention the drug addiction!

So you'll need cameras, will you?
More cameras than you can shake a criminal at!
More cameras to keep an eye on the cameras!
Then more cameras to keep an eye on the cameras that keep
an eye on the cameras!
And   so   forth.

As I,
George Orwell,
roll in my grave,
rhetoric and lies will roll from your tongues
as you roll out the blue carpet
and make preparations
for the totalitarian
state
visit.

TID

New Labour – Tories in disguise.
New Labour – with pound-signs in our eyes.
New Labour – Tories in disguise.
New Labour – Etonians spouting lies.

Devolution comes with a cost,
Teaching assistants in minimum-wage jobs.
Zero-hours contracts are now the norm.
Get off that picket line and ride the storm!
We'll shout rhetoric and see your families robbed;
We're the twenty-first-century Hand of God!

New Labour – Tories in disguise.
New Labour – with pound-signs in our eyes.
New Labour – Tories in disguise.
New Labour – Etonians spouting lies.

Devolution half-a-job Bobs,
Social care flogged to the dogs.
You're working-class?
We represent the *not-working class*.
We can only be trusted to stab you in the back
Whilst getting chummy with the right-wing hacks!

New Labour – Tories in disguise.
New Labour – we'll cut and privatise.
New Labour – Tories in disguise.
New Labour – with blue Etonian smiles.

THERE'S NO ONUS ON THE ONE PERCENT THAT OWN US

If I can stare at a blank canvas and see a thousand faces,
does that make me a shaman, or merely a visionary in the
making?
If I deformed my body, to make it permanently soulless,
would I be fit to walk in the shoes of the one percent that own
us?

'Cause, whether it's a fat banker's bonus
or a missed rent payment that leaves you homeless,
they lack the onus to tone down their venomous rage
exerted on the masses by the demonic state.

We've seen a thousand coffins, drunk a thousand wakes
as they continue to drone-strike Aleppo day by day,
then leave the parentless children in warzones to play
with cartridge shells and broken bones, a Syrian game of sticks
and stones.

'Cause, whether it's a fat banker's bonus
or that missed rent payment that leaves you homeless,
they lack the onus to tone down their venomous rage
exerted on the masses by the demonic state.

We're the one percent that own you!
Lobster shells, champagne flutes, cigars, expensive designer
suits.
We'll inflict 'equality' our own way.
Grammar schools versus welfare states.
Private-tutored DNA.
It's only limited access through these pearly gates!

Our halls are littered with the finest cocaine,
snuck in through customs at your expense.
But legalisation is utterly insane;
we wouldn't want the common folk to be able to claim
it like we do, as a legitimate expense!
We need three homes, plus one to rent!

So just donate those plebs a sleeping bag and tent,
then tell the beggars they ought've paid their rent,
then promptly remind them that they gave consent
for the one percent to own and govern them.

'Cause, whether it's a fat banker's bonus
or that missed rent payment that leaves you homeless,
they lack the onus to tone down their venomous rage
exerted on the masses by the demonic state.Snakes of Greed

She transfers nicotine into her lungs
via battered roll-up, bruised and canoed.

She's the envy of all the passin' lads
with odious beards and sleepin' bags,

victims of a shambles named *Universal Credit.*
Their universal bonus? They're all homeless tenants.

They're now ushered
from bank doorways, for not paying tax,

by snooty coppers
in riot vans.

The insult is palpable, considering the banks
avoid paying tax at every chance,

whilst our lives have been taxed and MOT'd
by policymakers: the Snakes of Greed.

If the homeless bleed our state,
then let the state bloody bleed.

We'd rather fund the homeless
than those Snakes of Greed.

A VISION OF THE FUTURE

I awake on my feet
queuing, in Walmart, for all my needs.

Health insurance, milk and bread.
                The bank account, to deposit
                    the paycheque.

I'll arrange the overdraft,
                then schedule my death
                for twenty years' time.

Whilst a wedding ceremony proceeds
on aisle nine,
                sweet vows are exchanged, in rapid time.

There's a funeral taking place on aisle six,
    so please don't make a big fuss over your new-wedded bliss.

Our honeymoon schedule is currently behind,
                so unfortunately your flight
                    won't arrive on time.

The dole queue is situated on aisle five.
                Under-twenty-ones to the back of the line.

                It's a 24/7 service, so you'll be seen
                    in good time.
A minimum wait of eight hours will suit you just fine.

                We have a special visitor in store today.
Kate from *Celebrity Shits in the Sink's*
here all day.

She'll be signing copies of her new book:
                Planting a Floater Whilst Peter Had a Look.

We stock all the latest flavours of the week,

from shabby-chic to chubby cheeks.
You can bet your bottom dollar
we stock all your *needs*.
We can even check your PPI whilst you sign the deeds.

The X Factor nation is at the gates, queuing in line to ensure
their place.
The BBC has filmed the lot,
and edited the story plot.
The game-show formula,
is no longer a game.
The TOWIE state has risen and trained

the Youth to think they're all born as stars – spray-tans,
steroids
and souped-up cars.

We stock all of your needs, under this roof – ready to
purchase,
without an ounce of truth.

The scientists have mocked
our lack of proof,
so we've deleted their channel from YouTube.

Now all that's left is what we sell – who needs heaven when we
offer hell?

You ought not to have questioned us; you ought not to have
questioned us.
We've a special aisle for you awkward lot –
on number four, our graveyard plot.

Walk into the void of napalm gas; we don't need a reason to
silence your ass!

So no more questions; just raise a smile
and celebrate capitalism's finest hour.

Your homely streets are now just aisles.
        Your homely streets are now just aisles.

We're the Walmart state of shopping aisles, brandishing synthetic
    smiles.

Your lovely home is now an aisle.
        Your lovely home is now an aisle.
Your lovely home is now an aisle.
        Your lovely home is now an aisle.

WYHTTBYLTH

Signed photographs of reptiles in monochrome frame.
Silver-spooned snakes versus
paltry-palmed pigs.
Intolerable followers of pure distaste.
Leaders who lack compassion
take first place.

A building site of droning tribes.
A Groundhog Day of sacrifice.
Bullet-bitten teeth of tarmac.
Gobshite singles paved in Marmite.
Loved or loathed, never in between.
Death-drenched, insidious.
Blooming wreaths
placed by dancers on the paupers' graves.
Your defiant welcomes have been outstayed.
Reality's not your friend, so please remain:
lovingly frowned upon or duly entertained.
A tourist plot, a diatribe,
an exhibit of razor blades.
There's always something in the way.
There's always something in the way.

Your bridal suite is now obsolete,
occupied by urchins in piss-stained briefs.
You commoners are all the same,
just chiselled down and victim-brained,
all sorry misplaced hurricanes,
just prairie folks on streets of rage.

A glamour pin-up, a sketched cartoon,
a Tutankhamun Looney Tune,
all arty-farty airs 'n' graces,
a broken pencil missing the pages.
Your chapped-lipped smile,
your balding hair,
your dungarees from Mothercare.

A vile king: a Tony Blair.
War criminals in serpents' lairs.
A newfound Tory in laboured glory
watching history repeat itself
as millions gamble with their health,
matchboxed in and ultra-stealth.
This class war's on and you're the game,
all liquored lips and nicotine stains.
Your fingernails are sinking ships.
Cast out those gullies, gyrate those hips.
The future kids'll shout remorse
from broken homes plagued by divorce,
the products of quick intercourse.
Poor Mam was Dad's weekend reward.
A fumbled hunk of stinking spunk:
the wealth of saved monopolies,
Etonian hypocrisies,
the glue of holed philosophies,
the bottled message seeking seas.

Come on now, men: just round them up,
these worthless sheep, into the scrubs,
the smallest fraction of Novocain
mixed with barbiturates
to numb their brains.
I FUCKING QUIT.
YOU FACKING QUIT?
Just yam a bowl of Weetabix.
Every true hero needs a fix,
an ounce of worth,
a fresh-pressed suit,
a lucky girl to play his flute.
Those songs you sing
redemption songs
of crooked vulture sing-alongs.
Have a row bend down for mass;
let our *blessed father* dry-pipe your ass!

You may well gasp!
You may well like
our Tory approach: a seatless bike
for thee who spies the unicorn
will deliver revenge served up lukewarm,
administered in staccato slingshot vowels.
No consonants, please, Carol;
I'm too worn out!

From this monochrome bliss
I'm a trapped goldfish,
this bloody world in which I swim.
Oh, praise the Lord, whoever he may be,
or maybe he's a dainty she?
We're sick and tired of your patriarchy;
it's got us nowhere, can't you see?
This world is done.
This world is dumb!
To your new world order I won't succumb.
It's one big messed-up monologue.
I often wonder how I carry on.
But I've got to win,
we've got to win
this fucking class war
we're living in.

SUITED AND BOOTED REPTILES

Is it all just snakes in suits, then?
he asks the ex-councillor.
Pretty much!
she replies,
rolling the note...
sniffing the line...

ACKNOWLEDGEMENTS

Versions of 'Bin Day/Autumn/Terraced Streets', 'Nineteen Eighty-Four Was Not an Instruction Manual' and 'Someone's Left Behind a Sovereign Ring' were previously published in editions of *Glove Zine*. 'A Vision of the Future' was originally published in *Razur Cuts Zine*. A version of 'At One with Nature' was originally published in *Here Comes Everyone* magazine. Versions of 'Nothing Ever Happens in Derby' and 'Our City Will Never Forget' were published in the Unislam 2019 anthology. Versions of 'Act 1', 'Our Man' and '#Identifying the Missing' originally appeared in the ACE-funded production Man Up, produced by RESTOKE. 'Our Man I' also appeared in the Morning Star. 'We Are Derby' was commissioned by Derby County Football Club and has appeared on the big screen at home games at Pride Park stadium since August 2018, as well as being featured on BBC Radio Derby, BBC Radio 5 Live and ITV Central.

*

I'd like to acknowledge you for buying/reading/borrowing/stealing this book; I hope you've enjoyed the journey, 'cause it nearly killed me! I'd also like to say thanks to anybody who's ever put me on at a gig/given me paid work and basically funded my poetry habit in any way!

Other shout-outs go firstly to Bridget, Clive, Harriet and the crew at Burning Eye Books for showing a great deal of patience with me during the compilation of this book. Next shout-outs go to my lovely wife and daughter Faye and Jessica, and the rest of my family and close friends, for putting up with me for all this time.

Special shout-outs to: Jim Mortram, Sophie Sparham, Trevor Wright, Casey Bailey, Anne Holloway and the Big White Shed crew, Henderson, Aimee and Sian @Writing East Midlands, Pete Stones @ACE, Miggy Angel, Keith Ford, Daron Carey, Rob True, Maria Ferguson, Matt Abbott, Toria Garbutt, Salena Godden, Sam Batley, Jordon, Sophie, Charles and Dylan @Idle Work Factory, Antony Owen, Simon Heywood, Moy McCrory, Joe Coghlan, Joshua Judson, Chip Hamer, Tim Wells, Anna

Saunders, Steve Pottinger, Emma Purshouse, Peter Raynard, Raymond Antrobus, Anthony Anaxagorou, Simon 'Praxis' Jones, Gavin Sibald, Stephen Battelle, Jyoti Mishra, Kev Keo, Blake Fallows, Owen Bradley, Hannah Swings, Helen Mort, Cash Carraway, Luke Kennard, Culture Matters, Martin Hayes, Dean Walker and Andrew Death (for enjoyable musical collaborations), my travelling band crew (Alex Blood, Gez Addictive, Gareth Ike), my fellow Unislam 2019 winning teammates and coaches (Memory Bhunu, Hannah Ledlie, Jonah Corren, Chloe Bettles, Anne Gill and Sean Colletti), my writing group at HMP Foston Hall, Clare, Paul and the RESTOKE crew, and all of my UP-MEN (without Man Up this book wouldn't exist).

To anyone I forgot – don't take it personally, I definitely didn't mean to!

I'd finally like to thank Matthew Clegg for his priceless advice when pulling together the final edits of these poems, and for telling me I might just be a poet, all of those years ago (even though you claim to not remember doing so.